AMENDMENTS TO THE UNITED STATES CONSTITUTION
THE BILL OF RIGHTS

PREVENTING CRUEL AND UNUSUAL PUNISHMENT

THE EIGHTH AMENDMENT

GREG ROZA

rosen publishing's
rosen central®

New York

Published in 2011 by The Rosen Publishing Group, Inc.
29 East 21st Street, New York, NY 10010

Copyright © 2011 by The Rosen Publishing Group, Inc.

First Edition

Library of Congress Cataloging-in-Publication Data

Roza, Greg.
The Eighth Amendment : preventing cruel and unusual punishment / Greg Roza. — 1st ed.
    p. cm. — (Amendments to the United States Constitution : the Bill of Rights)
Includes bibliographical references and index.
ISBN 978-1-4488-1263-9 (library binding)
ISBN 978-1-4488-2309-3 (pbk.)
ISBN 978-1-4488-2312-3 (6-pack)
1. Punishment—United States—Juvenile literature. 2. United States. Constitution. 8th Amendment—Juvenile literature. I. Title.
KF9225.R69 2011
345.73'077—dc22

Manufactured in the United States of America

CPSIA Compliance Information: Batch #W11YA: For further information, contact Rosen Publishing, New York, New York, at 1-800-237-9932.

On the cover: Left: A protester dressed as a prison inmate calls for the closing of the U.S. military prison at Guantánamo Bay in Cuba. Middle: A protester holds up a sign during an anti-death penalty rally. Right: Anti-death penalty activists gather for a rally outside the U.S. Supreme Court to mark historic court rulings on the issue.

CONTENTS

4 INTRODUCTION

7 **CHAPTER ONE**
PUNISHMENT IN
COLONIAL AMERICA

18 **CHAPTER TWO**
WRITING THE EIGHTH
AMENDMENT

29 **CHAPTER THREE**
DEFINING THE EIGHTH
AMENDMENT

40 **CHAPTER FOUR**
MODERN INTERPRETATIONS
OF THE EIGHTH AMENDMENT

53 AMENDMENTS TO THE
U.S. CONSTITUTION

56 GLOSSARY

57 FOR MORE INFORMATION

59 FOR FURTHER READING

61 BIBLIOGRAPHY

63 INDEX

INTRODUCTION

The Eighth Amendment to the Constitution was designed to protect people from the prosecutorial power of the U.S. government. Like the Fourth, Fifth, and Sixth amendments, the Eighth Amendment protects the rights of those accused of a crime. The Founding Fathers wanted to protect the citizens of the United States from the kind of government abuse and corruption they witnessed when England ruled the colonies.

However, the Eighth Amendment has long been considered the most poorly defined of the amendments in the Bill of Rights. The amendment reads: "Excessive bail shall not be required, nor excessive fines imposed, nor cruel and unusual punishments inflicted." For more

The last public hanging in the United States occurred on August 14, 1936, in Owensboro, Kentucky. Public anger eventually brought an end to this once-common method of execution.

than two hundred years, Americans have struggled to interpret and clarify the meanings of the phrases "cruel and unusual," "excessive bail," and "excessive fines."

The Founding Fathers had witnessed friends and patriots being captured by British authorities, held indefinitely without bail, and fined unreasonable sums of money. Others were tortured and put to death for their beliefs. They wanted to protect American citizens from unreasonable and malicious punishment.

The Eighth Amendment has endured over the years and continues to affect our lives today. Recent developments in the United States, such as the treatment of detainees held by the U.S. military in Guantánamo

Bay, Cuba, have once again brought the text of the Eighth Amendment under scrutiny. Many of the detainees were suspected terrorists believed to be a danger to American citizens. Held without the chance of bail, the detainees were also mistreated by some of their jailers and forced to participate in humiliating activities. While Americans are divided on this issue, many people have expressed their disapproval over what they consider cruel and unusual punishments occurring at Guantánamo, including a form of torture known as waterboarding. In 2008, the Supreme Court ruled that inmates of Guantánamo Bay were entitled to the protection of the U.S. Constitution.

CHAPTER ONE

PUNISHMENT IN COLONIAL AMERICA

L ife in the American colonies was not always easy for the colonists. This was particularly true for people accused of a crime. Colonists presumed to be guilty of a crime could be held without bail, forced to pay excessive fines, and subjected to "cruel and unusual" punishment. These punishments could range from torture and beatings to death. Death by hanging was the most common form of execution in the British colonies. Much like today, many people believed that corporal and capital punishment worked as a deterrent against crime, whereas others believed it to be inhumane. Many of the laws regarding fines, bail, and judicial punishments in the American colonies were directly influenced by British traditions.

Punishment in Eighteenth-Century Britain

By the time European colonies were established in North America, Britain already had a long history of harsh judicial sentences and excessive punishments. In eighteenth-century Britain, there were more than two hundred crimes for which capital punishment could be applied. These crimes included offenses as heinous as murder and rape and as minor as stealing a neighbor's animals and chopping down a tree.

Capital punishment is the execution or killing of a person by the state for his or her crimes; it is also referred to as the death penalty. The term "capital punishment" comes from the Latin word *capitalis*, which means "regarding the head." Originally, the term applied specifically to executions by decapitation, but today it applies to any execution. Crimes to which the death penalty may apply are known as capital offenses.

Capital punishment in Britain was often horrific. One of the worst capital punishments was hanging, drawing, and quartering. This monstrous punishment, used between 1283 and 1867, was reserved for those accused of treason.

This drawing depicts the hanging, drawing, and quartering of Guy Fawkes and those who helped him in his attempt to blow up the Houses of Parliament in 1605.

Convicted traitors were tied to wooden posts and "drawn" to their execution. After being hanged until they were nearly dead, they were then cut down, mutilated, beheaded, and their bodies were cut into four pieces, or quartered. The body was burned in public as a warning to others against

treason. Female traitors usually received a more "humane" sentence: they were burned at the stake or hung.

The British government also had a long list of offenses that could result in corporal punishment. Corporal punishment is the administration of pain as a punishment for breaking a rule or law. "Corporal" comes from the Latin word *corporalis*, meaning "body." This refers to the fact that pain is administered to the body. Once again, traitors were among the most heavily penalized. However, offenses such as theft and forgery were often treated with similarly severe punishments. These could include the amputation of a hand, cutting the nose, or branding.

Even when a criminal wasn't sentenced to death, corporal punishment in Britain was often barbaric. The accused often died, or came close to death. In 1630, for example, Puritan clergyman Alexander Leighton was charged with libel for writing a pamphlet that attacked the Anglican Church. Leighton was whipped so badly that he almost died. Then his hands and head were pilloried, or secured in a wooden restraint, and he was placed outside to be ridiculed by the public. His ear was nailed to the pillory, his cheek was branded, and his nose was slit; the next week he suffered that same fate on the opposite side of his face. After undergoing all of this, he was sentenced to life in prison and fined £10,000 ($15,282)—an enormous sum for the time.

Another common form of punishment was banishment. Some criminals were sent to the American colonies and forbidden to return to England for a period of time or return at all. Excessive fines and bail were also commonly imposed on those accused of a crime, particularly when the accused were wealthy. Excessive fines and bail could also be imposed on political hostages whose governments would pay to secure their safe return.

Punishment in the American Colonies

While punishment in the American colonies at this time was, relatively speaking, more humane than in England, it was still often very harsh. Hanging was the most common form of capital punishment in the colonies. Imprisonment was usually reserved for political hostages and criminals who had money to pay fines. Criminals who had no money were often put to death instead of imprisoned, as few colonists wanted to care for criminals who couldn't afford to pay for their own food and lodging.

In early American society, common forms of corporal punishment included pillorying, flogging, branding, and ear cropping. Some people

Pillorying involved securing someone in a wooden stockade—like the one shown here—for hours or even days. It was meant to cause pain and humiliation for the accused.

who were perceived to have committed a crime were subjected to torture, which was not considered cruel or unusual if it resulted in a confession. Forms of torture included the use of thumbscrews, starvation, and piling weights on the person's chest until he or she confessed. These methods were believed to be highly successful, but many people confessed to a crime they didn't commit simply to end the torture.

Salem Witch Trials

One of the most notorious accounts of cruel and unusual punishment in the British colonies is that of the Salem witch trials of 1692. The town of Salem, Massachusetts, was governed by laws of British tradition. They had strict laws against "consorting with the Devil." Superstitious fears would lead to one of our country's most heinous cases of cruel and unusual punishment.

Several factors contributed to the Salem witch trials. Salem was in a state of transition from an agricultural community to one based on sea trade and commerce. Tensions ran high as two groups of people struggled for control of the town. Illnesses such as small pox ran rampant. These factors put the people on edge and allowed the seeds of superstition and distrust to grow.

Defendants at the Salem witch trials were often humiliated before being sentenced to death. This 1853 painting shows the accused being forcefully stripped to show "the mark of the Devil" on her skin.

In 1692, the daughter and niece of Samuel Parris, a clergyman, developed a rare illness that caused them to act very strangely. Their illness may have been caused by food poisoning, but historians can't be certain. The doctor who treated them deduced that the cause was

supernatural. This resulted in a wave of paranoia in Salem, and residents began accusing people of witchcraft.

Between March 1 and September 22, 1692, thirteen women and six men were put on trial for witchcraft. The accused were given no rights, offered no bail, and subjected to humiliating and sometimes painful punishments. Even people who simply spoke out against the witch hunt were charged as accomplices. In the end, eighteen of the accused were put to death by hanging. One man was pressed to death under heavy stones for refusing to testify. In addition, many others—perhaps as many as two hundred people—were imprisoned without bail for witchcraft, and some died in jail. Two dogs were even executed as accomplices.

The fervor surrounding the Salem witch trials was extreme. Soon after the last defendant was put to death, many people denounced the trials. Several of the judges and jurors even confessed to being mistaken in their judgments.

Titus Oates

To begin to understand how laws regarding the treatment of the accused eventually transformed in the United States, we need to examine the case of Anglican priest Titus Oates, who lived in seventeenth-century England. During the late 1600s, he became the focus of a scandal in Britain. Oates—who had been arrested in the past for a long list of crimes, including public drunkenness and theft—was angered by the recent leniency that King Charles II had shown for Catholicism. In 1678, Oates reported a false account of a "Popish plot" planned by Catholics to assassinate Charles II, in which he mentioned many people by name. As a result, at least fifteen people Oates accused were put on trial and executed for treason.

Soon, however, it became clear that Oates had made up the story. Government officials confronted Oates, and he voiced his displeasure with the king and others in government. Eventually, he was fined £100,000 ($152,814) and put in prison. In 1685, James II—a Catholic—became King of England. James quickly had Oates retried for his crimes. He was found guilty of perjury for making false accusations against Catholics.

The judge presiding over the case noted that the death penalty was not a permissible punishment for perjury. Instead, he made up a punishment so harsh that many believed Oates would not survive. Oates' clerical status was stripped from him, he was heavily fined, and he was

This eighteenth-century drawing shows Titus Oates suffering public humiliation in a stockade. It's easy to see how people today might consider pillorying cruel and unusual.

sentenced to life in prison. In the weeks after he was convicted, Oates was subjected to frequent pillorying and public beatings. It was decreed that he would undergo the same punishment once a year. Cases like this one caused people to begin to rethink their beliefs in capital and corporal punishment.

Changing Perspectives

While judicial punishment in the colonies may sound cruel and unusual to us, the people of that era had a different perspective. Law enforcement in the colonies was not like it is today. People didn't have a police force to keep them safe. Jails and prisons were uncommon. It was much

AN EARLY HISTORY OF BAIL

The first British bail laws, which originated as far back as the thirteenth century, were frequently abused over the years. Bail and fines were often excessively high, and bail was frequently withheld altogether.

In the early seventeenth century, King Charles I expected certain nobles to give him loans. When they did not, he imprisoned them without bail or trial. Even when Parliament sought to create laws protecting the right to reasonable bail—as in the Petition of Right of 1628 and the English Bill of Rights of 1689—the king often found ways around the law.

Early U.S. bail laws were based on British laws and were often broken in similar fashion. Accused criminals were sometimes held without bail and trial for an indefinite period of time. Even after the Eighth Amendment became law, many people questioned exactly what "excessive bail" meant. Some argued that dangerous criminals did not deserve the right to bail, regardless of what the law said.

easier to commit a crime and get away with it. Therefore, many law-abiding citizens felt harsh punishments were just if they deterred crime.

In all likelihood, many colonists probably believed that a man like Titus Oates had received an appropriate punishment. Oates had, after all, been repeatedly convicted of a long list of crimes. Regardless, many colonists and British citizens in the late seventeenth century began to feel judicial punishment was often excessively barbaric and unfair. There were few standards regarding proper punishment and fines. The few laws there were regarding punishment, bail, and fines were often completely ignored by corrupt leaders. As the voices of the citizens grew louder, the governments started to listen and take action.

CHAPTER TWO

WRITING THE EIGHTH AMENDMENT

The American Revolutionary War between the American colonists and the British began in 1775. After years of fighting, the colonies won their independence from England, becoming the United States of America in 1783. The U.S. Constitution and the Bill of Rights, written soon after, represented a giant move away from British rule. However, the Founding Fathers were heavily influenced by British law documents. Two in particular greatly influenced the Eighth Amendment: the Magna Carta of 1215 and the Bill of Rights of 1689. These documents set limitations on the powers of the monarchy and increased the powers of Parliament, which represented the rights of the people.

THE ENGLISH INFLUENCE ON THE EIGHTH AMENDMENT

While several English documents have had a profound influence on the U.S. Constitution, none have had a greater influence on the Eighth Amendment than the Magna Carta and the English Bill of Rights. The Magna Carta states that, "For a trivial offence, a free man shall be fined only in proportion to the degree of his offence, and for serious offence correspondingly, but not so heavily as to deprive him of his livelihood." It goes on to say that, "A freeman shall be amerced [or have a fine imposed upon him] for a small offence only according to the degree of the offence; and for a grave offence he shall be amerced according to the gravity of the offence."

The specific text of the Eighth Amendment was taken directly from the English Bill of Rights. It states that, "Excessive bail ought not to be required, nor excessive fines imposed, nor cruel and unusual punishments inflicted." Together, these two English documents helped shape American laws regarding fines, bail, and punishments for convicted criminals.

The Magna Carta

In 1215, British nobles were upset with King John. They accused the king of imposing unfair taxes and using his position to place himself above the law. The nobles drafted a document and, with the backing of the Catholic Church, forced King John to sign it. The Magna Carta listed a set of laws based on earlier documents and traditional laws. It established that the king was not above the law.

The Magna Carta has had a major impact on the world through the years. It set the precedent of recording human rights in the form of laws. It also stated that a man accused of a crime should receive punishment equal to his crime in the form of an amercement, or a fine imposed as a punishment. In addition, the Magna Carta had a great influence on the U.S. Constitution.

The English Bill of Rights

In 1688, the Parliament (and angry citizens) forced King James II from the throne for abusing the powers of the monarchy. Parliament then asked the king's daughter Mary and her husband, William of Orange, to take the throne. However, Parliament also insisted that the new monarchs sign the English Bill of Rights. This document made Parliament more powerful than any single monarch. It also stated that the people had rights that the king and queen could not take away.

Shortly after the British Parliament passed the 1689 Bill of Rights, Titus Oates petitioned both Houses of Parliament—the House of Lords and the House of Commons—to release him from prison. He argued that his punishment was cruel and unusual and that his fine was excessive. However, the members of the House of Lords believed him to be insane and better off in prison. Furthermore, they believed his punishment was appropriate based on the fact that his actions led to the deaths of fifteen people. Many citizens felt the same way.

Regardless of what people thought about Oates and his crimes, a small group of people argued that the punishments imposed on him violated the English Bill of Rights. They believed his punishment would set a dangerous precedent, allowing Parliament to impose similarly barbaric punishments on others in the future.

Members of the House of Commons decided to release Oates. In speaking with the members of the House of Lords, they agreed that there was no precedent for the punishment in common law. They also believed that Oates's punishment set a bad example for future cases. If his punishment was not condemned as excessive, as well as cruel and unusual, what would stop Parliament from imposing similar punishments on people in the future? Oates was released soon after.

English Law Comes to America

In 1620, a small group of colonists in search of religious freedom left England and sailed for North America. They would come to be known as the Pilgrims. Before setting foot on solid land at Plymouth Rock in Massachusetts in 1620, the Pilgrims drafted a document known as the Mayflower Compact. This short document concerning the liberty of British citizens represents the first declaration of rights in the colonies.

Before the United States drafted the Constitution and became a free nation, colonial governments had their own constitutions. Most of them borrowed heavily from British documents, and many included clauses regarding bail, fines, and judicial punishment. For example, the 1641 Massachusetts Body of Liberties guaranteed bail to accused people, except for those charged with a capital crime or those charged with contempt of court.

With the signing of the Declaration of Independence in 1776, the Second Continental Congress called upon the colonial governments to establish their own constitutions. Many quickly answered the call. In Pennsylvania, government officials—led by Benjamin Franklin—drafted and signed the Pennsylvania Declaration of Rights. Partly based on earlier British documents, this unique document broadened the idea of what constituted a free man. The Pennsylvania Declaration of Rights stated that punishments should be "less sanguinary and in general more proportionate to the crime." This was just one of several

This painting by the artist Jean Leon Gerome Ferris shows his interpretation of the signing of the Mayflower Compact.

sections of the Pennsylvania Constitution that influenced leaders in other colonies, as well as the men who wrote the U.S. Constitution.

The Virginia Declaration of Rights of 1776

The first time the phrase "cruel and unusual punishment" was included in U.S. law was in the Virginia Declaration of Rights of 1776. This document was written by a wealthy landowner and political leader, George Mason. Mason was one of the most vocal opponents of British control in the colonies. In writing the Virginia

George Mason played an important role in American politics long before writing the Virginia Declaration of Rights. A justice of the Fairfax County court, he was elected to the Virginia House of Burgesses in 1759.

Declaration of Rights, Mason borrowed ideas from British documents and the works of British philosopher John Locke.

After several changes, some suggested by patriot and future president James Madison, the Virginia Declaration of Rights was approved. Many hailed it as the first document to truly uphold equality for all citizens. Mason's document influenced many others, including the declaration of rights of other states, the Declaration of Independence, and the 1789 French Declaration of the Rights of Man and Citizen.

The U.S. Constitution and the Bill of Rights

Shortly after the colonies had drafted their own declarations of rights, the young nation's finest thinkers gathered in Philadelphia, Pennsylvania, to draft the U.S. Constitution. They drew upon previously written documents, including the Magna Carta and the Virginia Declaration of Rights.

The U.S. Constitution advocated a strong federal, or central, government. However, some of America's leaders felt that the document gave the federal government too much power. They wanted to change, or amend, the Constitution to ensure that the federal government would not be more powerful than individual state governments.

The men who felt the Constitution should be ratified without the Bill of Rights were called Federalists, and they included Alexander Hamilton, James Madison, and John Jay (the authors of the Federalists Papers). The men in favor of adding a Bill of Rights were called Anti-Federalists, and they included Patrick Henry and Samuel Adams. George Mason even refused to sign the Constitution if it didn't include a declaration of rights. Eventually, Anti-Federalist concerns were addressed by the addition of the Bill of Rights to the U.S. Constitution.

Although the Bill of Rights was written by James Madison, it was heavily influenced by George Mason. Fifty years after the Bill of Rights was written, Thomas Jefferson said, "The fact is unquestionable that the Bill of Rights and the Constitution of Virginia were drawn originally by George Mason." The Bill of Rights was hailed as a historic and truly groundbreaking political document.

The Eighth Amendment

One of the primary Anti-Federalist concerns was the treatment and rights of the accused. This is reflected in the Fourth through Eighth amendments.

Artist Peter F. Rothermel's painting *Patrick Henry Before the Virginia House of Burgesses* depicts Patrick Henry speaking out against the Stamp Act on March 23, 1775.

Many of the Founding Fathers felt it was important to include a law against cruel and unusual punishment. Others, however, thought the amendment was too vague to be truly effective. They argued that "excessive" and "cruel and unusual" could mean different things to different people.

The men who drafted the U.S. Constitution took the language for the Eighth Amendment from the Virginia Declaration of Rights. However, Mason suggested an important change. The Virginia Declaration of Rights stated that "excessive bail ought not be required, nor excessive fines imposed, nor cruel and unusual punishment inflicted." Mason wanted the language of the Eighth Amendment to be more direct. He changed it to: "Excessive bail shall not be required, nor excessive fines imposed, nor cruel and unusual punishment inflicted." By changing "ought not" to "shall not," Mason hoped to create a stronger, more effective law.

As with the English laws that came before it, the Eighth Amendment does not specifically define what punishments are cruel and unusual. Nor does it define what is meant by excessive. The men who wrote the Bill of Rights left the task of defining the Eighth Amendment to the states and future generations.

The Judiciary Act of 1789

Some critics of the new Constitution argued that while the Eighth Amendment clearly protected citizens from excessive bail, it did not necessarily protect them from the refusal of bail. It quickly

The Judiciary Act of 1789 was ratified three days after the Bill of Rights. The text of the act states, "And upon all arrests in criminal cases, bail shall be admitted, except where the punishment may be death."

became clear that the Eighth Amendment required further legislation to help define the meaning of "excessive" so that it covered both the amount of bail as well as the right to have it at all.

On September 24, 1789—just three days after the Bill of Rights was ratified—the U.S. Congress passed the Judiciary Act of 1789. This act established the structure of the U.S. court system, including the Supreme Court and smaller judicial districts. It also outlined the crimes for which bail could be offered and set limits on bail amounts. The act stated that bail would be available to those accused of any noncapital crime. For capital offenses, the decision to grant bail would be left up to the judge presiding over the case. Although the Supreme Court would be called upon to reassess the meaning of the Eighth Amendment as well as the Judiciary Act of 1789, federal bail law would remain largely untouched for the next 177 years.

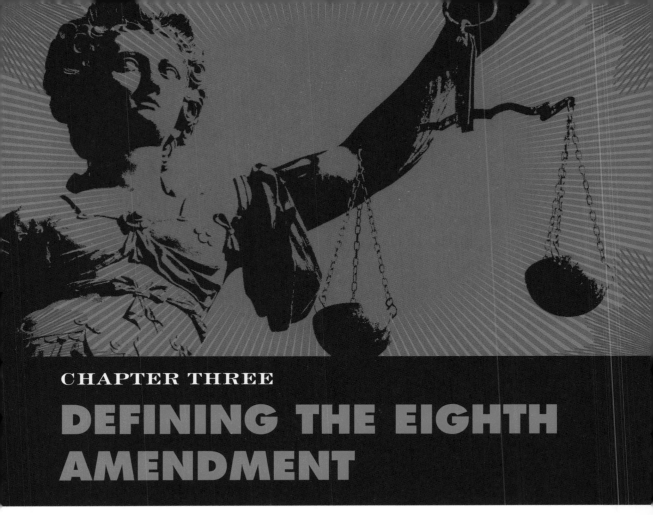

CHAPTER THREE

DEFINING THE EIGHTH AMENDMENT

Despite the rights guaranteed by the Eighth Amendment, common punishments of the late eighteenth century remained in practice for many years to follow. These included pillorying, whipping, and branding. The punishment for robbery sometimes included thirty-nine lashes with a whip. Today in the United States, these punishments would certainly be considered cruel and unusual. But two hundred years ago, they were acceptable. In fact, many people believed they were necessary.

Slavery remained legal in the United States for seventy-five years after the U.S. Constitution was ratified. Many of the same people who

This drawing was used for the seal of the Society for the Abolition of Slavery in England in the 1780s. It later appeared on broadsides in the United States with the antislavery poem "Our Countrymen in Chains."

fought for freedom and equality denied slaves those same basic rights. Slaves were routinely subjected to beatings, torture, and execution. The growing abolition movement sought to draw attention to the cruel and unusual punishment that many slaves had to endure, but slavery was an industry that remained entrenched in the American economy for years to come. The people that the Constitution defined as citizens did not include slaves, indentured servants, women, or people who didn't own land. It would take decades for the U.S. government and the American people to embrace a new, more humane way of thinking.

Slow Reform

Throughout the nineteenth century, the American perspective on what was excessive, cruel, and unusual punishment began changing. As Americans began making more money and the country grew richer, the idea of what an excessive fine amounted to changed.

One reason for the slow changes was that the Eighth Amendment pertained to the federal government, and criminal punishments were handled primarily by state governments. Federal criminals were held in state prisons or county jails; the first federal prisons weren't built until 1891. Each state took a different approach to the issue of criminal punishment. Some states outlawed the death penalty, while others felt it was necessary to deter crime.

In the early 1800s, some groups spoke out against corporal and capital punishment. Most of the developments regarding the death penalty occurred at the state level, and punishments were rarely considered cruel and unusual by state courts. In the early 1800s, most states began passing laws that restricted the use of capital punishment to only the most heinous crimes, particularly rape, murder, and treason. Public whipping

was outlawed in 1839. In 1852, Rhode Island became the first state to outlaw the death penalty. Wisconsin followed in 1853. Other states abolished the death penalty as well, but over time, most of them reinstated it.

Allan Pinkerton (*left*), President Abraham Lincoln (*center*), and Major General John A. McClernand (*right*) pose for a photo in Antietam, Maryland, on October 3, 1862.

However, attempts at reform met many obstacles. Much of the nation, including the federal government, was focused on the burgeoning abolition movement, the Civil War, and the period of Reconstruction that followed. For example, President Abraham Lincoln suspended the rights of prisoners during the Civil War, allowing military leaders to arrest civilians and hold them indefinitely without the benefit of a fair trial. Many saw this as unconstitutional, while others felt it was a necessary act in a time of war.

Wilkerson v. Utah

During the nineteenth century, the Supreme Court made very few rulings that affected the meaning of the Eighth Amendment. The first significant case regarding cruel and unusual punishment occurred in 1878.

The law in the Utah Territory at that time stated that the punishment for a convicted murderer was death by firing squad or hanging. Wallace Wilkerson, a man convicted of murder and sentenced to death by firing squad, argued that this method of execution constituted cruel and unusual punishment. He appealed the territory's decision to execute him in this way.

The U.S. Supreme Court denied Wilkerson's appeal. It believed that since the firing squad did not entail a form of torture before death, it could not be considered cruel and unusual. The court ruled that "cruel and unusual punishments are forbidden by the Constitution, but ... the punishment of shooting as a mode of executing the death penalty for the crime of murder in the first degree is not included in that category, within the meaning of the Eighth Amendment." Wilkerson was executed by firing squad on May 16, 1879. Despite the ruling that death by firing squad was not cruel or unusual, reports say Wilkerson suffered for twenty-seven minutes before he finally died.

This case marked an end to the federal government's silence regarding the Eighth Amendment. Furthermore, it validated a decision regarding capital punishment made at the state level. Other important changes would follow in the years to come.

Against Public Executions

By the 1890s, many states had passed laws limiting the number of criminal offenses subject to capital punishment. However, it wasn't until 1897 that the federal government officially limited capital offenses to treason, murder, and rape. It also decided that a jury had the power to rule that the defendant was guilty of a capital offense without imposing a capital punishment; instead, a guilty verdict could result in a life sentence.

Another gradual change was the shift away from public executions, which were often witnessed by large crowds. Executions in the United States had long been a public affair and were intended to serve as a warning for other criminals. By the 1830s, many death penalty opponents were beginning to speak out against public executions, especially hangings, which could result in a slow, agonizing death. It wasn't until the 1890s that the Supreme Court suggested that public executions should be given up in favor of controlled executions with a limited number of spectators. This decision was made in hopes of "civilizing" capital punishment.

The Supreme Court's decision on the matter of public executions took many years to catch on at the state level across the nation. One of the last public executions occurred on August 14, 1936, in Owensboro, Kentucky. This execution was a public hanging attended by about twenty thousand people. Eighteen months after it occurred, the Kentucky State Legislature passed a law banning public executions.

The Supreme Court Rules on Electrocution

In another attempt to make capital punishment more humane, officials in New York State suggested the use of electricity to execute criminals. The first person sentenced to the electric chair was William Kemmler of Buffalo, New York. In 1889, Kemmler killed his common-law wife with a hatchet. After sentencing, Kemmler challenged the ruling, stating that electrocution qualified as cruel and unusual punishment. It is important to note that Kemmler challenged the method of execution but not the death penalty itself.

In 1890, the Supreme Court ruled that a method of execution could not be deemed cruel and unusual, or considered a form of torture, as long as it is quick and humane. Specifically, the court decided that electrocution, although untested on humans, was a humane form of execution. The ruling set a precedent regarding the Eighth Amendment. It said that the death penalty itself was not cruel or unusual, but the method of execution could be. Since this ruling, no method of execution has been deemed unconstitutional by the Supreme Court.

The electric chair was introduced as a method of execution in the United States in 1890. Today, execution by electric chair is legal in only nine states.

While the Supreme Court stood by this ruling, the first electrocution certainly seemed cruel and unusual to many who witnessed it. Kemmler was knocked unconscious by the first jolt, but it would take three more jolts and ten more minutes until he was pronounced dead. Future electrocutions were held in private.

Weems v. United States

The 1910 case *Weems v. United States* marked the first time that the Supreme Court overturned a criminal sentence because it believed it inflicted cruel and unusual punishment. Federal employee Paul Weems was accused of falsifying government documents. He was sentenced to fifteen years of hard labor and excessive fines, in addition to other punishments.

The Supreme Court overturned the ruling, deciding that the severity and duration of the punishment was not in proportion to the crime, which was relatively minor. Justice Joseph McKenna stated that an understanding of cruel and unusual punishment "is not fastened to the obsolete but may acquire meaning as public opinion becomes enlightened by humane justice. . ." In other words, Justice McKenna was stating that the meaning of the Eighth Amendment transforms as a society grows and becomes more enlightened. The *Weems* ruling marked a turning point in our interpretation of the Eighth Amendment.

Bail and Fines

To this day, there is no uniform set of rules governing bail. Each state has its own set of guidelines. Furthermore, judges can set an excessively high bail, or even deny bail altogether, if they feel the defendant could pose a risk to the community if set free. Some feel this is a violation of the Eighth Amendment.

CRITERIA FOR SETTING BAIL

When setting bail for a defendant, a court considers several issues. These include:

- The seriousness of the crime
- The weight of evidence against the accused, or the amount of proof linking the accused to the crime
- The ties that the accused has to the community where he or she will be put on trial
- The ability of the accused to pay a given amount of bail
- The chances that the accused will flee the area if released

These criteria help the court set a bail that is fair and proportionate to the charges being brought against the accused.

Fines imposed by judges can be overturned if a court of appeals rules that the judge abused his or her discretion in imposing inappropriately large fines. However, this rarely occurs.

Stack v. Boyle

The first reassessment of the meaning behind the excessive bail clause did not occur until 1951—162 years after the Judiciary Act of 1789 was passed. That year, twelve people were arrested and charged with violating the Smith Act, which made it an offense to belong to an association that advocated the violent overthrow of the U.S. government. At first, each defendant received a different bail amount, ranging from $2,500 to $100,000. Then, bail was set at $50,000 for each defendant. In the case of *Stack v. Boyle*, the defendants attempted to have the bail lowered on the grounds that it was excessive according to the Eighth Amendment. The district court denied the motion, as did a court of appeals.

The Supreme Court found that the bail amount was much higher than previous amounts for similar cases and that the district court did not explain the reason why. The Supreme Court ruled that a bail of $50,000 was excessive, given the limited financial resources of the defendants and the lack of proof that the defendants would flee before their trial. This ruling defined what "excessive bail" means today.

CHAPTER FOUR

MODERN INTERPRETATIONS OF THE EIGHTH AMENDMENT

We have a different view of the Eighth Amendment than eighteenth-century Americans did. Our understanding of what constitutes cruel and unusual or excessive punishment has been influenced by years of criminal cases and judicial rulings. However, Americans are still divided over the true meaning of the Eighth Amendment, especially when it comes to capital punishment.

In 1958, the Supreme Court ruled on the case of *Trop v. Dulles*. In 1944, U.S. Army private Albert Trop escaped from a U.S. Army jail in Morocco. He turned himself in the next day. After a military trial, Trop was sentenced to three years' hard labor and loss of pay. He was also dishonorably discharged from the army.

Before Earl Warren became chief justice of the Supreme Court in 1953, he served three terms as the governor of California. He had also served as California's attorney general.

In 1958, Trop applied for a U.S. passport; he was denied it. It was ruled that because Trop had deserted the army, he lost his U.S. citizenship. Trop went to court in hopes of having his citizenship reinstated, but several courts ruled against him. Eventually, Trop's case reached the Supreme Court, which ruled that stripping Trop of his citizenship was cruel and unusual punishment and therefore unconstitutional. Chief Justice Earl Warren said, "The words of the [Eighth] Amendment are not precise, and their scope is not static. The Amendment must draw its meaning from the evolving standards of decency that mark the progress of a maturing society." Warren meant that it is up to contemporary society to dictate what the meaning of the Eighth Amendment should be. It's important to consider these words when discussing modern-day interpretations of the Eighth Amendment.

Francis v. Resweber

In 1946, sixteen-year-old Willie Francis was convicted of murder in Louisiana and sentenced to death by electric chair. Due to a malfunction with the equipment, Francis received a shock but did not die. While authorities were planning a second date of execution, Francis's lawyer appealed to the Supreme Court, saying that to attempt to execute Francis a second time would be cruel and unusual punishment and therefore unconstitutional.

In the case of *Francis v. Resweber*, the Supreme Court ruled 5–4 that sending Francis to the electric chair a second time did not violate the Constitution. Francis was successfully executed in May 1947. While the Supreme Court decided not to overturn the conviction, one of the dissenting justices who heard the case, Justice Harold Burton,

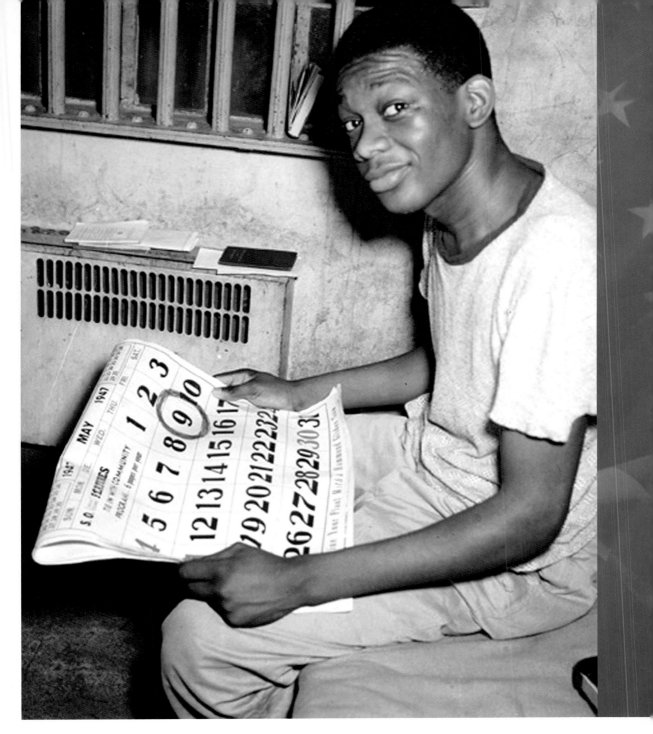

While sitting in his jail cell, Willie Francis holds a calendar with a circle around May 9— the date of his second scheduled execution.

believed that the Eighth Amendment should apply to the states. Burton wrote:

> It is unthinkable that any state legislature in modern times would enact a statute expressly authorizing capital punishment by repeated applications of an electric current separated by intervals of days or hours until finally death shall result. . . . Although the failure of the first attempt, in the present case, was unintended, the reapplication of the electric current will be intentional. How many deliberate and intentional reapplications of electric current does it take to produce a cruel, unusual, and unconstitutional punishment?

This marked the first time the court assumed that the Eighth Amendment applied to the states.

Capital Punishment

At the time of this writing, Amnesty International reported that while 137 countries had outlawed capital punishment, it was still legal in 61 countries, including the United States. As of 2010, fifteen U.S. states and the District of Columbia have outlawed the death penalty. Although capital punishment is legal in the rest of the states, many seldom use it. Other states, particularly Texas, are known to make liberal use of the death penalty.

The Supreme Court has made several key rulings on the use of capital punishment. Some rulings reduced or banned the use of capital punishment for youthful offenders, and others banned its use on the mentally disabled. However, two cases in particular were perhaps most influential in shaping the use of the death penalty in contemporary American society: *Furman v. Georgia* and *Gregg v. Georgia*.

THE EIGHTH AMENDMENT IN ACTION: ROBINSON v. CALIFORNIA

In 1962, the Supreme Court made its first ruling officially applying the Eighth Amendment to the states in the case *Robinson v. California*. At the time, California law imposed a mandatory prison sentence for substance addiction. However, the Supreme Court ruled that imprisonment (ninety days in this case) for a misdemeanor was cruel and unusual punishment and therefore unconstitutional. The court decided that drug addiction was an illness, and it was unfair to imprison a person simply for being ill, even for a single day. The ruling specified that being addicted to a substance was not the same as selling, buying, or possessing an addictive substance, which were all illegal offenses.

The *Robinson* case also marks the first instance when the Supreme Court ruled that the Fourteenth Amendment covered cruel and unusual punishment. Adopted after the Civil War, the Fourteenth Amendment offers a broad interpretation of U.S. citizenship. Section One of this amendment states that "no State shall make or enforce any law which shall abridge the privileges or immunities of citizens of the United States." According to the Supreme Court's ruling, the actions of the California state government were cruel and unusual and infringed upon the rights and freedoms of a U.S. citizen. The Supreme Court has not yet ruled that the Fourteenth Amendment applies to bail and fines.

Furman v. Georgia

In 1972, the Supreme Court reconsidered capital punishment in the *Furman v. Georgia* ruling. *Furman v. Georgia* was actually three cases involving three defendants, all sentenced to the death penalty by a jury. William Furman shot (many say accidentally) the homeowner of a house he was burglarizing, and Lucius Jackson and Elmer Branch were found guilty of rape in unrelated cases. All three defendants were African American men. This, to many opponents of the death penalty, indicated that capital punishment had a racial bias to it.

On June 29, 1972, the Supreme Court ruled 5–3 to reverse all three convictions. They declared that the death penalty was cruel and unusual punishment when applied to these cases. While the ruling itself was rather short, each of the five concurring justices wrote a lengthy statement explaining their personal motives. Several of the justices mentioned racial bias as a contributing factor in their decision. They argued that the use of the death penalty was based solely on the decision of a jury, making it both "capricious" and "arbitrary." Others stated that the death penalty was an outdated method of punishment.

The four dissenting judges also wrote individual statements. Chief Justice Warren Burger argued that the death penalty had been ruled cruel and unusual because it was so rarely used. He stated that one way for states to make the death penalty constitutional would be to put more criminals on death row, thereby making capital punishment less rare. Some critics have commented that Burger was actually offering states a way to get around the ruling. Shortly after the verdict, thirty-five states passed new death penalty laws in an attempt to preserve the death penalty.

In his statement regarding the *Furman v. Georgia* decision, Justice William Brennan—one of the five concurring judges—declared that there are four principles that help determine if a punishment is cruel and unusual:

- A punishment must not by its severity be degrading to human dignity, especially torture.

- A severe punishment that is obviously inflicted in wholly arbitrary fashion.

- A severe punishment that is clearly and totally rejected throughout society.

- A severe punishment that is patently unnecessary.

In his opinion, these principles proved that the death penalty is in fact unconstitutional.

Gregg v. Georgia

The 1976 Supreme Court case *Gregg v. Georgia* actually involved five separate murder cases. *Gregg v. Georgia* concerned a man named Troy Gregg who was convicted of murder and robbery in a hitchhiking case in Georgia. Under Georgia's revised death penalty laws, a jury first sentenced Gregg to the death penalty, and then an appellate court reviewed the ruling.

By a vote of 7–2, the Supreme Court ruled, in all five cases, that the states had sufficiently changed their laws to ensure that the death penalty could no longer be considered capricious or arbitrary. The seven concurring judges believed that because so many states had revised their death penalty laws, capital punishment was clearly a socially acceptable form of punishment for murders and was therefore not cruel and unusual.

During *Furman v. Georgia*, the Supreme Court ruled that current state death penalty laws were unconstitutional because a jury verdict alone could result in a death sentence. Four short years later, *Gregg v. Georgia* changed all this. The case prompted the states to revise their death penalty laws, which in turn allowed the Supreme Court to redefine the death penalty as constitutional. This outcome has not ended the arguments and controversy surrounding capital punishment, but it has shaped our contemporary understanding of the Eighth Amendment.

Opponents of the death penalty hold a rally in front of the U.S. Supreme Court building in Washington, D.C., on June 30, 2006—the thirtieth anniversary of the *Gregg v. Georgia* ruling.

The Bail Reform Act of 1966

In 1966, the Supreme Court made the first major change to federal bail law since the Judiciary Act of 1789. The Bail Reform Law of 1966 made the appearance of the defendant at his or her trial the main criteria for granting bail to those charged with noncapital offenses. Courts were instructed to release defendants with the least amount of burden possible to ensure that they show up at their trial. The act did not allow judges to take the chance of danger to people or property into account when setting bail, except for cases involving the death penalty. The Bail Reform Act drew a great deal of criticism. Cases of violent crimes committed by defendants while they were released on their own recognizance increased.

The Bail Reform Act of 1984

The Bail Reform Act of 1984 changed the 1966 act to allow judges to refuse bail to defendants who posed a threat to the community. Defendants accused of committing violent crimes, crimes requiring a maximum sentence of life imprisonment or death, or drug offenses for which the maximum conviction is greater than ten years, repeat felony offenders, or defendants that pose risks of flight, obstruction of justice, or witness tampering could be refused bail. Defendants that do not fit any of these criteria must be offered bail.

In 1986, this act was challenged during the Supreme Court case *United States v. Salerno*. Anthony Salerno was being held on racketeering charges. He was denied bail because officials believed that he would commit more crimes, including murder, if he was released. Salerno successfully appealed his case to the U.S. Court of Appeals, which declared the 1984 act unconstitutional.

Anthony "Fat Tony" Salerno is shown here leaving jail on February 27, 1985, after posting bail. On November 19, 1986, Salerno was convicted of racketeering and sentenced to one hundred years in prison.

The Supreme Court overturned the decision 6–3. Justice William Rehnquist wrote that the Bail Act of 1984 does not violate the excessive bail clause of the Eighth Amendment. He stated that, "Nothing in the text of the Bail Clause limits permissible government considerations solely to questions of flight." Rather, he added, governments should have the right to deny bail to anyone who poses a risk to the community.

Excessive Fines

Federal law states that no one may carry more than $10,000 cash out of the United States without reporting it to a customs official. In 1998, defendant Hosep Bajakajian was detained at Los Angeles International Airport for attempting to take $357,144 out of the country without filling out the appropriate paperwork. Both a federal district court and a federal appeals court ruled that Bajakajian had to forfeit all of the money he was carrying with him at the time of the arrest.

In the case *United States v. Bajakajian*, the Supreme Court ruled 5–4 that the federal officials had violated the excessive fines clause of the Eighth Amendment. The ruling stated that the "amount of the forfeiture was grossly disproportionate to the gravity of the defendant's offense." This case marks the most significant Supreme Court ruling regarding the excessive fines clause of the Eighth Amendment.

The Eighth Amendment Today

Today, Americans are as divided about the Eighth Amendment as they were in 1789. Take, for example, the argument for corporal punishment in schools. In 1977, the Supreme Court ruled that it was legal for students in U.S. schools to receive corporal punishments (specifically, paddling). Similar verdicts have been given regarding corporal punishment for criminals in prison. Many think it is perfectly fine, while others find it unconstitutional.

Despite differences in Americans' opinions, Supreme Court rulings over the past fifty or sixty years have helped solidify our understanding of what the Eighth Amendment means. This includes not only cases the Supreme Court has overturned, but also cases the Court declined to reverse. As a nation, we have become more humane and fair regarding the rights of the accused. We can thank the Framers of the Constitution for having the foresight to protect our most basic rights, even for those who may have broken the law. The Eighth Amendment has served to protect the freedoms enjoyed by American citizens. We will surely hear more on these issues as American beliefs and thoughts on the Eighth Amendment continue to transform in the years to come.

AMENDMENTS TO
THE U.S. CONSTITUTION

First Amendment (proposed 1789; ratified 1791): Freedom of religion, speech, press, assembly, and petition

Second Amendment (proposed 1789; ratified 1791): Right to bear arms

Third Amendment (proposed 1789; ratified 1791): No quartering of soldiers in private houses in times of peace

Fourth Amendment (proposed 1789; ratified 1791): Interdiction of unreasonable search and seizure; requirement of search warrants

Fifth Amendment (proposed 1789; ratified 1791): Indictments; due process; self-incrimination; double jeopardy; eminent domain

Sixth Amendment (proposed 1789; ratified 1791): Right to a fair and speedy public trial; notice of accusations; confronting one's accuser; subpoenas; right to counsel

Seventh Amendment (proposed 1789; ratified 1791): Right to a trial by jury in civil cases

Eighth Amendment (proposed 1789; ratified 1791): No excessive bail and fines; no cruel or unusual punishment

Ninth Amendment (proposed 1789; ratified 1791): Protection of unenumerated rights (rights inferred from other legal rights but that are not themselves coded or enumerated in written constitutions and laws)

Tenth Amendment (proposed 1789; ratified 1791): Limits the power of the federal government

Eleventh Amendment (proposed 1794; ratified 1795): Sovereign immunity (immunity of states from suits brought by out-of-state citizens and foreigners living outside of the states' borders)

Twelfth Amendment (proposed 1803; ratified 1804): Revision of presidential election procedures (electoral college)

Thirteenth Amendment (proposed 1865; ratified 1865): Abolition of slavery

Fourteenth Amendment (proposed 1866; ratified 1868): Citizenship; state due process; application of Bill of Rights to states; revision to apportionment of congressional representatives; denies public office to anyone who has rebelled against the United States

Fifteenth Amendment (proposed 1869; ratified 1870): Suffrage no longer restricted by race

Sixteenth Amendment (proposed 1909; ratified 1913): Allows federal income tax

Seventeenth Amendment (proposed 1912; ratified 1913): Direct election to the U.S. Senate by popular vote

Eighteenth Amendment (proposed 1917; ratified 1919): Prohibition of alcohol

Nineteenth Amendment (proposed 1919; ratified 1920): Women's suffrage

Twentieth Amendment (proposed 1932; ratified 1933): Term commencement for Congress (January 3) and president (January 20)

Twenty-first Amendment (proposed 1933; ratified 1933): Repeal of Eighteenth Amendment (Prohibition)

Twenty-second Amendment (proposed 1947; ratified 1951): Limits president to two terms

Twenty-third Amendment (proposed 1960; ratified 1961): Representation of the District of Columbia in electoral college

Twenty-fourth Amendment (proposed 1962; ratified 1964): Prohibition of restriction of voting rights due to nonpayment of poll taxes

Twenty-fifth Amendment (proposed 1965; ratified 1967): Presidential succession

Twenty-sixth Amendment (proposed 1971; ratified 1971): Voting age of eighteen

Twenty-seventh Amendment (proposed 1789; ratified 1992): Congressional compensation

Proposed but Unratified Amendments

Congressional Apportionment Amendment (proposed 1789; still technically pending): Apportionment of U.S. representatives

Titles of Nobility Amendment (proposed 1810; still technically pending): Prohibition of titles of nobility

Corwin Amendment (proposed 1861; still technically pending though superseded by Thirteenth Amendment): Preservation of slavery

Child Labor Amendment (proposed 1924; still technically pending): Congressional power to regulate child labor

Equal Rights Amendment (proposed 1972; expired): Prohibition of inequality of men and women

District of Columbia Voting Rights Amendment (proposed 1978; expired): District of Columbia voting rights

GLOSSARY

accomplice A person who helps someone commit a crime.

appeal A request for, and the hearing of, a previously tried case that can result in a new verdict.

appellate court A court with the power to review and reverse the decisions of lower courts.

bail An amount of money that is paid to release a person who has been arrested with the understanding that the accused will appear at a court trial at a future date.

contempt The failure to respect the authority of the court.

deterrent Something that dissuades a person from doing something.

dissent To disagree with.

judicial Relating to a body of judges or the system that administers justice.

legislative Relating to a body of lawmakers or the system of lawmaking.

libel Making false statements that damage someone's reputation.

misdemeanor A crime less serious than a felony that results in less severe punishment.

pillory A wooden frame with holes in which someone's head and hands could be locked.

precedent An action or ruling used to justify future actions and rulings.

proportionate Having the correct relationship of size, quantity, or degree to something else.

racketeering To make money from illegal activities.

recognizance A formal agreement made before a judge to do something, such as show up for a trial after paying bail.

treason The betrayal of one's country.

FOR MORE INFORMATION

American Civil Liberties Union (ACLU)
Capital Punishment Project
Durham, NC 27701
(919) 682-5659
Web site: http://www.aclu.org
The Capital Punishment Project is a national program of the ACLU that conducts public education, advocates reform, and represents defendants convicted of capital crimes.

Amnesty International
777 UN Plaza, 6th floor
New York, NY 10017
(212) 867-8878
Web site: http://www.amnesty.org
Amnesty International is a worldwide association that campaigns for internationally recognized human rights for all.

Death Penalty Information Center (DPIC)
1101 Vermont Avenue NW, Suite 701
Washington, DC 20016
(202) 289-2275
Web site: http://www.deathpenaltyinfo.org
The DPIC is a nonprofit organization that provides the media and public with analysis and information about capital punishment.

Supreme Court of the United States
One First Street NE

Washington, DC 20543
Web site: http://www.supremecourtus.gov
The Web site for the U.S. Supreme Court allows users to browse documents and past cases.

Web Sites

Due to the changing nature of Internet links, Rosen Publishing has developed an online list of Web sites related to the subject of this book. This site is updated regularly. Please use this link to access the list:

http://www.rosenlinks.com/ausc/8th

FOR FURTHER READING

Andrews Henningfeld, Diane. *The Death Penalty*. Farmington Hills, MI: Greenhaven Press, 2006.

Aronson, Marc. *The Real Revolution: The Global Story of American Independence*. Boston, MA: Houghton Mifflin Harcourt, 2005.

Branscomb, Leslie Wolf. *Supreme Court Justices: Earl Warren*. Greensboro, NC: Morgan Reynolds Publishing, 2011.

Day, Nancy. *The Death Penalty for Teens: A Pro/Con Issue*. Berkeley Heights, NJ: Enslow Publishers, 2000.

Devaney, Sherri. *The Death Penalty*. Yankton, SD: Erickson Press, 2007.

Dudley, William, ed. *The Death Penalty: An Opposing Viewpoints Guide*. Farmington Hills, MI: Greenhaven Press/Thomson-Gale, 2006.

Edge, Laura B. *Locked Up: A History of the U.S. Prison System*. Minneapolis, MN: Twenty-First Century Books, 2009.

Fradin, Dennis. *The Bill of Rights*. Tarrytown, NY: Marshall Cavendish, 2008.

Fradin, Dennis. *The U.S. Constitution*. Tarrytown, NY: Marshall Cavendish, 2007.

Giddens-White, Bryon. *The Supreme Court and the Judicial Branch*. Chicago, IL: Heinemann-Raintree, 2005.

Herda, D. J. *Furman v. Georgia: The Death Penalty Case*. Berkeley Heights, NJ: Enslow Publishers, 2010.

Hinds, Maureen J. *Furman v. Georgia and the Death Penalty Debate: Debating Supreme Court Decisions*. Berkeley Heights, NJ: Enslow Publishers, 2005.

Leavitt, Aime Jane. *The Bill of Rights in Translation: What It Really Means*. Mankato, MN: Capstone Press, 2008.

Pederson, Charles E. *The U.S. Constitution & Bill of Rights*. Edina, MN: ABDO Publishing, 2010.

Smith, Rich. *Eighth Amendment: The Right to Mercy*. Edina, MN: ABDO Publishing, 2008.

Sobel, Syl. *The Bill of Rights: Protecting Our Freedom Then and Now*. Hauppauge, NY: Barron's Educational Series, 2008.

Taylor-Butler, Christine. *The Constitution of the United States*. Danbury, CT: Children's Press, 2008.

Whitcraft, Melissa. *The Mayflower Compact*. New York, NY: Children's Press, 2003.

Yero, Judith Lloyd. *The Mayflower Compact*. Washington, DC: National Geographic Society, 2006.

BIBLIOGRAPHY

Bodenhamer, David J., and James W. Ely Jr., eds. *The Bill of Rights in Modern America*. Bloomington, IN: Indiana University Press, 2008.

Claus, Laurence. "The Anti-Discrimination Eighth Amendment." *Harvard Journal of Law and Public Policy*, Vol. 28. Retrieved January 20, 2010 (http://ssrn.com/abstract=600242).

Epstein, Lee, and Thomas G. Walker. *Constitutional Law for a Changing America: Rights, Liberty, and Justice*. Washington, DC: CQ Press, 2004.

Freedman, Russell. *In Defense of Liberty: The Story of America's Bill of Rights*. New York, NY: Holiday House, 2003.

Gaines, Larry K., and Roger LeRoy Miller. *Criminal Justice in Action*. Belmont, CA: Thomson Wadsworth, 2009.

Hudson, David L. *The Bill of Rights: The First Ten Amendments of the Constitution*. Berkeley Heights, NJ: Enslow Publishers, 2002.

Jasper, Margaret C. *The Law of Capital Punishment*. New York, NY: Oxford University Press, 2008.

Kukathas, Uma, ed. *Death Penalty*. Farmington Hills, MI: Greenhaven Press, 2008.

Linder, Douglas. "The Witchcraft Trials in Salem: A Commentary." UNKC School of Law, September 2009. Retrieved January 20, 2010 (http://www.law.umkc.edu/faculty/projects/ftrials/salem/SAL_ ACCT.HTM).

Melusky, Joseph A., and Keith A. Pesto. *Cruel and Unusual Punishment: Rights and Liberties Under the Law*. Santa Barbara, CA: ABC-CLIO, Inc., 2003.

New York Times. "Six Men Legally Killed." May 17, 1879. Retrieved January 29, 2010 (http://query.nytimes.com/mem/archive-free/pdf?res=9A0CE5DC133EE63BBC4F52DFB3668382669FDE).

Patrick, John J. *The Bill of Rights: A History in Documents.* New York, NY: Oxford University Press, 2003.

Prinalgin. "George Mason and the Bill of Rights." Associated Content, April 10, 2006. Retrieved January 24, 2010 (http://www.associated content.com/article/26713/george_mason_and_the_bill_of_rights.html?cat=37).

Stinneford, John F. "The Original Meaning of 'Unusual': The Eighth Amendment as a Bar to Cruel Innovation." *Northwestern University Law Review*, Vol. 102, No. 4, 2008. University of Florida Levin College of Law Research. Paper No. 2009-26 (http://papers.ssrn.com/sol3/papers.cfm?abstract_id=1015344).

U.S. Supreme Court. "*Furman v. Georgia*, 408 U.S. 238 (1972)." FindLaw. Retrieved February 2, 2010 (http://caselaw.lp.findlaw.com/scripts/getcase.pl?court=US&vol=408&invol=238).

U.S. Supreme Court. "Louisiana ex rel. *Francis v. Resweber* (No. 142) Affirmed. J. Burton, Dissenting Opinion." Cornell University Law School Supreme Court Collection. Retrieved January 31, 2010 (http://www.law.cornell.edu/supct/html/historics/USSC_CR_0329_0459_ZD.html).

U.S. Supreme Court. "*Trop v. Dulles* (No. 70) 239 F.2d 527, reversed." Cornell University Law School Supreme Court Collection. Retrieved January 29, 2010 (http://www.law.cornell.edu/supct/html/historics/USSC_CR_0356_0086_ZO.html).

U.S. Supreme Court. "*Wilkerson v. Utah*, 99 U.S. 130 (1878)." FindLaw. Retrieved January 29, 2010 (http://caselaw.lp.findlaw.com/cgi-bin/getcase.pl?court=US&vol=99&invol=130).

INDEX

B

bail laws, history of, 4–6, 7, 10, 16, 27–28, 37–39, 49–51
Bail Reform Act of 1966, 49
Bail Reform Act of 1984, 49–51
Bill of Rights, 4, 18, 24, 27, 28

C

capital punishment, 5, 7, 8, 11, 14, 16, 31, 32, 34–37, 40, 42–47
corporal punishment, 10, 11–12, 16, 29, 31

E

electrocution, 35–37, 42–44
English Bill of Rights, 18–19, 20–21

F

Francis v. Resweber, 42–44
Furman v. Georgia, 45–47

G

Gregg v. Georgia, 47

H

hanging, drawing, and quartering, 8–10

J

Judiciary Act of 1789, 28, 38

M

Magna Carta, 18–20, 24

O

Oates, Titus, 14–16, 17, 20–21

P

punishment
  in the American colonies, 11–14
  in eighteenth-century Britain, 8–10, 14–17

R

Robinson v. California, 45

S

Salem witch trials, 12–14
slavery, 29–31
Stack v. Boyle, 38–39

T

Trop v. Dulles, 40–42

U

United States vs. Bajakajian, 51
United States vs. Salerno, 49–51

V

Virginia Declaration of Rights, 23, 24, 27

W

Weems v. United States, 37
Wilkerson v. Utah, 33–34

About the Author

Greg Roza has been creating educational materials for schools and libraries for ten years. He has a master's degree from SUNY Fredonia. Roza lives in Hamburg, New York, with his wife, Abigail, and their children Autumn, Lincoln, and Daisy.

Photo Credits

Cover (left) Nicholas Kamm/AFP/Getty Images; cover (middle) William Thomas Cain/Getty Images; cover (right) Tim Sloan/AFP/Getty Images; p. 1 (top) © www.istockphoto.com/Tom Nulens; p. 1 (bottom) © www.istockphoto.com/Lee Pettet; p. 3 © www.istockphoto.com/Nic Taylor; pp. 4–5 Newsmakers/Getty Images; pp. 7, 18, 29, 40 © www.istockphoto.com/arturbo; pp. 8–9, 15, 23 Hulton Archive/Getty Images; p. 11 Lake County Museum/Getty Images; pp. 12–13 The Bridgeman Art Library/Getty Images; p. 22 SuperStock/Getty Images; p. 25 Fotosearch/Getty Images; pp. 26–27 www.ourdocuments.gov; pp. 30, 31–32 Library of Congress Prints and Photographs Division; p. 36 Doulgas Doig/Evening Standard/Getty Images; p. 41 Pictorial Parade/Getty Images; p. 43 © AP Images; p. 48 upiphotos/Newscom.com; p. 50 NY Daily News Archive/Getty Images.

Photo Researcher: Amy Feinberg